Positive *Cooking*

Members Favourite
Classic
Recipes

Classic Contents

Lighter Bites

Chicken & Poultry

Pork & Bacon

Beef & Lamb

Budget Meals

Meat-free Menu

Members are always telling us how much they enjoy simple, tasty recipes they can easily prepare either when eating solo or with family and friends.

So, by popular demand, we have put together this collection of "Classic" favourites. Some are your favourites from past Eating Plans which you have asked us to revive, and some are new recipes which we have no doubt will become firm favourites of the future.

All recipes have been counted to fit into the Positive Eating Plan. You'll find calories, Checks and fat gram values for all recipes - minus "free" foods, of course! Most recipes also include "serving suggestions", and we give separate counts when these are added to the recipe. We also tell you what type of meal it is, for those of you who prefer to "Choose Meals" rather than "Choose Checks".

Do check out the "Free Foods" list and "Classic" Check List so you can include even more variety and add those essential personal touches.

Enjoy - we're sure you will!

• Calories Checks Fat Grams

Free Foods

Herbs and spices may be used freely on the Positive Eating Plan, as long as they don't have added oil.

Small quantities of seasonings such as soy sauce, beef or yeast extract, stock cubes and a light spray of oil are also "free".

Whenever "free" salad or vegetables are mentioned, you may choose from the following:

Alfalfa sprouts	French beans (greenbeans)
Artichoke hearts	Jerusalem artichokes
Asparagus	Kale
Aubergine	Leeks
Baby sweetcorn	Lettuce, all types
Bamboo shoots	Mangetout/snow peas
Beansprouts	Marrow
Beetroot	Mooli
Bok choi/pak choi	Mushrooms
Broccoli	Okra
Brussels sprouts	Onions, all types
Cabbage, all types	Peppers, all colours
Calabrese	Pumpkin
Carrots	Radishes
Cauliflower	Runner beans
Celeriac	Salsify
Celery	Sauerkraut
Chard	Spinach
Chicory	Spring greens
Chinese leaves	Squash, all types
Christophene (cho-cho)	Sugar snap peas
Courgettes	Swede
Cress	Tomatoes
Cucumber	Turnips
Endive	Water chestnuts
Fennel	Watercress

Remember - "free" foods do not need to be counted on the Positive Eating Plan!

Item			
1 small slice bread	50	2	0.5
1 medium slice bread	80	3	1
50g bread roll or crusty bread	125	5	2
100g small potato	70	3	0
150g medium potato or 4-5 small new potatoes	105	4	0
200g medium-large potato	140	6	0.5
300g large potato	210	8	1
75g parsnip	50	2	1
1 rounded tbsp fresh or frozen peas	20	1	0.5
1 rounded tbsp frozen or canned mixed vegetables	20	1	0
1 rounded tbsp frozen or canned sweetcorn	30	1	0.5
1 medium apple or pear	50	2	0
100g strawberries or raspberries	25	1	0
Rhubarb		free food	
1 medium egg	80	3	6
30g half-fat cheddar	80	3	4
30g Edam	95	4	7
1 level tbsp single cream	30	1	3
1 level tbsp double cream	70	3	7
1 tsp low-fat spread	20	1	2
1 tsp butter	35	1.5	4
1 level dspn cornflour	25	1	0
1 rounded tsp sugar	20	1	0
1 dspn Oxo or Bisto Best Gravy Granules	20	1	0
1 dspn apple sauce	10	0.5	0
1 dspn brown sauce or tomato ketchup	15	0.5	0
1 dspn low-calorie mayonnaise	30	1	3

nb: values are typical averages across brands and types

Classic
Posh Potato Salad

Serves 1

per serving   150   6 3

150g/5 oz potato
2 tbsp sliced green beans
1-2 spring onions, sliced
1 tbsp fat-free natural fromage frais
1 tbsp low-calorie mayonnaise

Boil the potato, adding the green beans towards the end of cooking. Drain and allow to cool.

Chop the cooked potato and mix with the green beans and spring onions.

Mix together the fromage frais and mayonnaise and stir into the potato and vegetables.

Serving suggestions

Posh Potato Salad is ideal served with lean cold meat or fish and "free" salad. Here are a few ideas with counts you need to add to the above. All would be ideal as a Quick Meal :

60g/2 oz lean pastrami	75	3	2
60g/2 oz lean boiled or roast ham	100	4	4
60g/2 oz lean roast topside of beef	90	4	3
1 skinless chicken breast	140	6	2
75g/2½ smoked salmon	90	4	3

Classic
Boston Beans

Serves 1

per serving   300 **12** (9)

or 1 Quick Meal

1 small onion, chopped
Spray oil
2 rashers rindless, streaky bacon
200g small can baked beans in tomato sauce
1 tsp treacle or brown sugar
1 tsp soy sauce
1 tsp mustard
Worcester sauce, to taste (optional)
Granulated sweetener, to taste (optional)

Soften the onion in a small saucepan sprayed with oil.
Meanwhile grill the bacon until crisp, then chop.

Stir beans into the onions. Add chopped bacon, treacle or
brown sugar, soy sauce, and mustard. Heat through, stirring
continuously.

Taste and add a few drops of Worcester sauce if you prefer
things spicy, and/or granulated sweetener if you prefer a
sweeter taste.

Tip: *This recipe makes a good accompaniment at a barbecue -
you can double or quadruple the quantities. If using a normal
serving spoon (rather than a 15ml measuring tablespoon)*

per spoonful   50 **2**

classic
Sardine & Lemon Pâté

Serves 1

per serving   200   **8**

120g can sardines in brine, drained
1-2 dspn lemon juice, to taste
2 rounded dspn fat-free fromage frais
2 dspn chopped parsley
Black pepper

Remove backbones from sardines, if preferred.* Mash sardines with lemon juice and blend with fromage frais. Stir in chopped parsley and season with black pepper.

* If bones are left in, they provide a good source of calcium. Sardines are also an excellent source of healthy omega 3 fats.

Serving suggestion

To make melba toast, toast 2 medium slices wholemeal bread on both sides. Remove crusts and discard. Slice through the centre of each piece of toast (to reveal bread inside). Cut into triangles and toast the bread side.

Serve the pâté and toast accompanied by "free" salad and lemon wedges.

per serving :   300   **12**

or 1 Quick Meal

nb: if you eat the crusts, add 50 cals or 2 Checks!

Classic
Savoury Toasted Cheese

Serves 1

per serving   170 **7** 5

or 1 Breakfast

| 30g/1 oz half-fat cheddar, grated |
| 1 tbsp fat-free natural fromage frais |
| 1 spring onion, sliced |
| 1 medium slice bread |
| Grilled tomato halves to serve |

Mix together the cheddar, fromage frais and spring onion.

Toast the bread on one side. Spread cheese mixture on untoasted side and grill.

Serve with grilled tomatoes.

Classic
Loose Meat Sandwich

per serving   250   **10** 8

or 1 Booster Quick Meal

60g/2 oz lean beef mince
30g/1 oz chopped onion
1 dspn tomato ketchup
1 tsp mustard, or to taste
1 burger bun
"Free" salad to serve

Dry-fry the mince with the chopped onion. Drain any surplus fat.

Stir in the ketchup and mustard.

Toast the burger bun.

Serve the mince over the two burger bun halves, accompanied by "free" salad.

classic
Garlic Mushrooms & Prawns

Serves 1

per serving   125   **5** (5)

| 6 mushrooms |
| Black pepper |
| 60g/2 oz prawns, defrosted if frozen |
| 30g (quarter of 125g tub) Boursin Light |
| Garlic & Herbs soft cheese |

Pre-heat oven to 180°C/gas mark 4.

Slice mushrooms and place on a square of foil, large enough to make a parcel. Season with black pepper. Mix in prawns and top with dabs of soft cheese.

Make foil into a secure parcel and bake in oven 10-12 minutes, or until juices just start to run.

Serving suggestion

Bake or microwave a 200g/7 oz potato. Serve mushrooms and prawns over potato, accompanied by "free" salad.

per serving :   275   **11** (6)

or 1 Quick Meal

classic
Duck in Cherry Sauce

Serves 2

per serving   250 **10** 8

| 2 duck breasts |
| 2 rounded tbsp reduced-sugar morello cherry jam |
| 4 tbsp red wine |

Pre-heat oven to 190°C/gas mark 5.

Lift skin almost completely away from breasts. Remove the thick layer of fat from under the skin. Lay skin back over breasts. Pierce with a fork. Roast breasts on a rack approximately 45 minutes or until juices run clear.

Warm jam and wine together in a small saucepan, stirring until jam has dissolved. Boil to reduce and thicken.

Discard skin from duck, cut breasts into thick slices, arrange on a serving dish and pour over cherry sauce.

Serving suggestion

Boil 300g/10 oz new potatoes. Serve each person with one duck breast, half the sauce, half the new potatoes and a selection of steamed "free" vegetables.

per serving :   355 **14** 8

or 1 Booster Main Meal

Classic
Creamy British Turkey Tagliatelle

Serves 4

per serving   400   **16**   7

or 1 Main Meal

200g/7 oz tagliatelle
Spray oil
450g/1 lb turkey stir-fry strips
100g/3½ oz lean back bacon, chopped
1 medium onion, peeled and sliced
115g/4 oz button mushrooms, sliced
2 tbsp grated rind from unwaxed lemon
200g pot fat-free fromage frais
Salt and freshly ground black pepper
2 tbsp freshly chopped parsley or torn basil
4 dspn grated parmesan cheese

Cook the tagliatelle in lightly salted boiling water until just tender. Drain.

Fry turkey in pan sprayed with oil approximately 3 minutes, or until sealed.

Add the onion and bacon and continue to cook for 3 minutes, stirring frequently.

Add the mushrooms, lemon rind and stir-fry for 3 minutes.

Turn down heat and stir in the fromage frais and seasoning. Heat very gently 1-2 minutes. Stir in the parsley or basil.

Serve each person with one-quarter of the tagliatelle, quarter of the turkey sauce and top with 1 dspn grated parmesan cheese.

classic
Sesame Chicken & Apricot Rolls

Serves 4

per roll   145   **6** 5

4 skinless and boneless chicken thighs
8 ready-to-eat semi-dried apricots
4 tsp sesame seeds
4 wooden cocktail sticks

Pre-heat oven to 180°C/gas mark 4.

Open out thighs and flatten them a little with a meat mallet or heavy knife handle. Place 2 apricots on each thigh, roll up and secure with a wooden cocktail stick.

Roll each thigh in 1 tsp sesame seeds and place on a non-stick baking tray. Bake 30 minutes. Remove cocktail sticks when cool enough to handle.

Serving suggestions

Serve each person with 2 warm rolls, 150g/5 oz new potatoes and "free" vegetables.

per serving :   395   **16** 10

or 1 Main Meal

or

Allow rolls to cool completely. Store in fridge. Serve each person with 2 cold rolls, cut into slices with "free" salad

per serving :   290   **12** 10

or 1 Quick Meal

Classic
Chicken, Ham & Sweetcorn Pie

Serves 4

per serving

350 **14** 7

or 1 Booster Main Meal

500g/18 oz potatoes, peeled
45g/1½ oz cornflour
2 chicken Oxo cubes
575ml/1 pint skimmed milk
225g/8 oz cooked chicken, chopped
115g/4 oz lean ham, chopped
4 rounded tbsp sweetcorn
2 tbsp chopped parsley
Spray oil
"Free" vegetables to serve

Boil potatoes. Drain, cool and slice.

Pre-heat oven to 220°C/gas mark 8.

Put cornflour and crumbled Oxo cubes into a saucepan. Stir in milk and bring to the boil, stirring continuously until sauce thickens. Remove from heat.

Place chopped chicken, ham, sweetcorn and parsley in an ovenproof dish. Stir in white sauce. Arrange potato slices over mixture and spray lightly with oil. Bake 20 minutes, then finish off under a hot grill to brown potatoes.

Serve each person with one-quarter of the recipe accompanied by "free" vegetables.

Classic
Chicken in Wine & Mushroom Gravy

Serves 2

per serving 200 **8** 2

2 skinless chicken breasts
60g/2 oz chopped onion or shallot
Spray oil
1 small glass white wine
1 chicken Oxo cube dissolved in 100ml/3½ fl.oz hot water
1 rounded tsp tomato purée
Pinch of dried tarragon, thyme or Herbes de Provence
6 mushrooms, sliced
1 tsp cornflour (optional)

Cook chicken breasts and onion or shallot over moderate heat in a pan sprayed with oil. Cook about 8-10 minutes, stirring onions frequently and turning over breasts after about 4 or 5 minutes.

Add wine and allow to bubble up. Stir in chicken stock, tomato purée and herbs. Cover and simmer 10 minutes. Add mushrooms and cook uncovered 5 minutes.

If you prefer, gravy may be thickened by mixing cornflour with 1 tbsp water. Stir into gravy and cook 1 minute.

Serving suggestion

Boil and mash 450g/1 lb potatoes with a little skimmed milk. Serve each person with 1 chicken breast and half the gravy accompanied by half the mash, green beans and baby carrots or other "free" vegetables.

per serving : 375 **15** 3

or 1 Main Meal

Classic
Californian-Style Chicken

Serves 2

per serving   225   **9** **2**

2 skinless chicken breasts
Spray oil
1 small clove garlic, crushed
4 tbsp fresh orange juice
½ chicken stock cube
2 dspn marmalade
1 tsp white wine vinegar

Spray pan with oil and heat. Cook chicken breasts over medium heat approximately 20 minutes or until cooked through. Turn over halfway through cooking. Remove and keep warm.

Add garlic to pan and heat 1 minute. Stir in orange juice, ½ stock cube, marmalade and wine vinegar. Bring to the boil stirring continuously, until stock cube has dissolved and sauce has slightly thickened.

Serve sauce poured over chicken breast.

Serving suggestion

Boil 85g/3 oz white and wild mixed rice. Serve each person with 1 chicken breast and half the sauce with half the rice and steamed broccoli and mangetout, or other "free" vegetables.

per serving :   375   **15** **3**

or 1 Main Meal

Classic
Paprika Pork Roast

Serves 6

per serving   200   **8**   7

Recipe used with kind permission of British Meat

900g/2lb* boned and rolled, rindless, pork leg joint
1 large, juicy lemon
3-4 sprigs fresh thyme
2 rashers lean back bacon
1 dspn paprika

* If buying a joint with rind on, choose one weighing approx. 1kg -1.1 kg/approx. 2lb 4-6 oz. This will weigh around 900g/2lb when rind is removed.

Pre-heat oven to 180°C/gas mark 4.

Place joint on a rack in a roasting tin. Slice half the lemon and arrange on top of the joint together with the thyme and bacon.

Squeeze juice from the other half of the lemon, mix with the paprika and drizzle over the joint.

Roast, uncovered, approx. 1½ hours for medium, or 1¾ -2 hours for well done.

Serving suggestion

Peel, boil and mash 1.2kg/2lb 10 oz sweet potatoes with a little skimmed milk, salt and plenty of black pepper. Serve one-sixth of the joint to each person together with one-sixth of the sweet potato mash and purple sprouting broccoli or other "free" vegetables.

per serving :   375   **15**   8

or 1 Main Meal

Classic
Pork & Pineapple Casserole

per serving   225   **9** 6

2 x 150g/5 oz lean, trimmed pork steaks
Salt & pepper
1 small red or green pepper, chopped or sliced
227g can of 4 pineapple rings in juice
1 tbsp Oxo or Bisto Best chicken gravy granules

Pre-heat oven to 190°C/gas mark 5.

Season the pork steaks and grill 3 minutes on each side.

Place steaks in an ovenproof casserole together with the peppers, pineapple rings and juice. Cover and bake approximately 45-60 minutes, until steaks are tender.

Place pork steaks, pineapple and peppers onto serving plates. Quickly stir the gravy granules into the casserole juices to thicken.

Serving suggestion

Boil and mash 350g/12 oz potatoes. Serve each person with half the casserole, half the mashed potatoes and 2 rounded tbsp peas or mixed vegetables.

per serving :   400   **16** 7

or 1 Main Meal

Classic
Apple & Onion Spare Rib Chops

Serves 2

per serving   250   **10**

2 x 175g/6 oz spare rib/shoulder pork chops (choose the leanest you can find)
Salt and pepper
1 medium onion, sliced
1 small apple

Pre-heat oven to 170°C/gas mark 3.

Place the chops in a roasting tray. Season with salt and pepper. Top with onion slices.

Peel, core and slice the apple into rings and place these on top of the onions. Cover tightly with foil and bake approximately 1½ hours, or until chops are very tender. Drain off all fat before serving.

Serving suggestion

Boil and mash 350g/12 oz potatoes. Make gravy from 2 dspn Oxo or Bisto Best chicken gravy granules and 150ml/5 fl.oz boiling water. Serve each person with 1 chop, half the onion and apple, half the mash and gravy, and cabbage and carrots or other "free" vegetables.

per serving :   400   **16**

or 1 Main Meal

classic
Pork & Apricot Pilaff

per serving   400   **16**   7

or 1 Main Meal

1 tsp low-fat spread
100g/3½ oz lean stir-fry pork strips
1 small onion, finely sliced
Pinch of cinnamon
½ chicken Oxo cube
200ml/⅓ pint hot water
60g/2 oz rice
3 fresh apricots (or canned in juice), stoned and sliced
"Free" vegetables to serve

Melt the low-fat spread in a small saucepan and cook the pork strips and onion slices 3-5 minutes, stirring frequently. Add the cinnamon and cook a few seconds more.

Dissolve the Oxo in the hot water. Add rice to pan, then stir in the stock.

Cover and simmer gently approximately 15 minutes. Add apricots and continue to cook a further 10 minutes, or until liquid has been absorbed.

Serve with "free" vegetables.

Classic
Fidget Pie

per serving   400   16 6

or 1 Main Meal

275g/10 oz potato
1 medium onion
1 medium eating apple
2 rashers lean, trimmed back bacon
Pepper
275ml/½ pint chicken stock
Lightly steamed cabbage to serve

Pre-heat oven to 180°C/gas mark 4.

Peel and slice the potato and onion thinly. Peel core and slice the apple. Chop the bacon.

Layer the potato, onion, apple and bacon in an ovenproof dish, seasoning with pepper and finishing with a layer of potatoes.

Pour over the chicken stock and bake covered 30 minutes. Remove cover and bake a further 15-20 minutes to brown top.

Serve with lightly steamed cabbage or other "free" vegetables.

Classic
Sweet & Sour Gammon

Serves 4

per serving   200   **8**

4 x lean, trimmed gammon steaks, approx. 115g/4 oz each
1 level tbsp cornflour
1 tbsp vinegar
1 tbsp soy sauce
1 tbsp tomato purée
275ml/½ pint unsweetened orange juice
Granulated sweetener (optional)

Grill the gammon steaks.

Place the cornflour into a saucepan. Mix in the vinegar, soy sauce and tomato purée. Stir in the orange juice.

Bring to the boil, stirring continuously until sauce thickens.

Serve sauce poured over grilled gammon.

Serving suggestion

Either bake or microwave 4 x 275g/10 oz potatoes in their jackets, or boil 250g pack Sharwood's medium or thick egg noodles.

Serve each person with 1 gammon steak, one-quarter of the sauce, 1 jacket potato or quarter of the noodles and "free" vegetables either boiled, or stir-fried in spray oil (add a little water or stock to prevent sticking).

per serving :   400   **16**

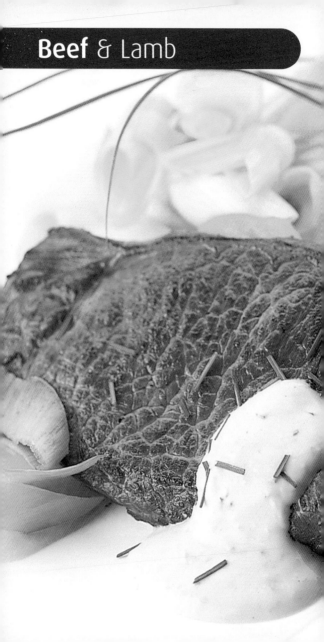

Classic
Creamy Garlic Steak

per serving   275   **11**

Recipe used with kind permission of British Meat

2 x 150g/5 oz lean rump steaks
Salt and pepper
Spray oil (optional)
60g/2 oz low-fat garlic & herb soft cheese (e.g. Boursin Light)
6 tbsp skimmed milk
Salt and pepper

Season steaks and grill to your liking under a pre-heated grill.

Put soft cheese and milk into a small saucepan and heat gently about 1-2 minutes, stirring continuously. Remove from heat immediately it starts to thicken. Season to taste. Serve steaks topped with sauce.

Serving suggestion

Serve each person with 1 steak topped with half the sauce, 150g/5 oz new potatoes, broccoli and asparagus tips, or other "free" vegetables.

per serving :   380   **15** ⑪

or 1 Main Meal

Steak Fajitas in Potato Skins

Serves 2

per serving 300 **12** 6

or 1 Quick Meal
or 1 Booster Main Meal

300g/10 oz lean rump steak
1 green pepper
1 red pepper
1 small onion
115g/4 oz mushrooms
2 x 275g/10 oz potatoes, boiled or microwaved in their jackets
Spray oil
1 tsp chilli powder, or to taste
Pinch of cumin
Salt and black pepper
"Free" salad to serve

Pre-heat oven to 220°C/gas mark 8.

Cut the steak into strips. Cut the peppers into strips. Slice the onion and mushrooms. Cut the cooked jacket potatoes in half. Scoop out the centres leaving a thin shell of potato. (Discard centres or save for another recipe.) Spray shells lightly with oil and bake approximately 20 minutes or until crispy.

Stir-fry the steak strips in pan sprayed with oil. Set aside.

Add vegetables to pan and stir-fry 3-4 minutes. Sprinkle in chilli powder and cumin and stir-fry 1 minute more. Return meat to pan with 1 tbsp water and stir 2-3 minutes more. Season to taste.

Serve each person with 2 potato skins filled with the steak and vegetable mixture accompanied by "free" salad.

classic
Beef in Stout with Filo Nests

Serves 4

per serving 400 **16** (11)

or 1 Main Meal

600g/1¼ lb trimmed weight, lean stewing steak
Spray oil
2 large onions, sliced
350g/12 oz carrots, sliced
4 sticks celery, sliced
1 clove garlic, peeled and crushed
330ml/good ½ pint stout, e.g. Guinness
1 tsp thyme
1 beef stock cube
3 rounded tbsp tomato purée
Salt and pepper
Water as required
4 x 45g/1½ oz sheets Jus-rol filo pastry
"Free" vegetables to serve

Cut the steak into chunky cubes. Spray a large saucepan with oil, heat and brown the steak on all sides in two or three batches. Set aside.

Add a little water to the pan and scrape up the meat juices. Add onions and cook until soft and lightly browned. Cover with lid between stirs. Add water if necessary.

Return meat to pan together with carrots, celery, garlic, stout, thyme, crumbled stock cube and tomato purée. Stir and bring to the boil. Turn heat down very low, cover and simmer gently approximately 2½ - 3 hours. Check about every half hour. Stir in a little water if dry. Season to taste.

Pre-heat oven to 200°C/gas mark 6. Spray one side of each sheet of filo with oil. Scrunch up each sheet into a nest, approx. 10cm/4 inches diameter. Place on a baking sheet, oiled side up and bake approximately 10-15 minutes or until golden. Serve each person with quarter of the beef topped with 1 filo nest, accompanied by "free" vegetables.

Classic
Minced Beef
& Vegetable Hotpot

Serves 1

per serving   350   **14**   12

or 1 Booster Main Meal

1 small onion
1 medium carrot
1 stick celery
115g/4 oz lean minced beef or minced steak
1/2 tsp mixed herbs
200g/7 oz potato, washed
175ml/6 fl.oz beef stock
"Free" vegetables to serve

Pre-heat oven to 190°C/gas mark 5.

Peel and chop the onion, carrot and celery. (Other "free" vegetables may be used if preferred). Mix with the minced beef and herbs.

Slice the potato thinly (does not have to be peeled). In an ovenproof casserole, layer the potato slices with the meat and vegetable mixture, finishing with a layer of potatoes. Pour over stock, cover tightly and bake approximately 1 hour.

Serve accompanied by "free" vegetables.

classic
Lamb Chops Veracruz

400 **16** (11)

or 1 Main Meal

1 small onion or shallot, finely chopped
400g can tomatoes
½ tsp chilli powder, or to taste
100g/3½ rice
150ml/¼ pint lamb or beef stock
1 green pepper, chopped
1 tbsp raisins
4 lamb chops, trimmed of all visible fat
"Free" vegetables to serve

Pre-heat oven to 190°C/gas mark 5.

Place the chopped onion or shallot in a microwavable and ovenproof casserole with 1 tbsp water and microwave 1-2 minutes, or until softened.

Add the tomatoes, chilli powder, rice, stock, peppers and raisins. Stir together, breaking up the tomatoes. Add the chops, cover and bake 45-60 minutes, or until lamb and rice are cooked through.

Serve 2 chops and half the rice mixture to each person, accompanied by "free" vegetables.

classic
Marinated Lamb Steaks

Serves 4

per serving · · · · · · 275 ·

275ml/½ pint unsweetened orange juice
1 dspn fresh lime juice
2 tbsp chopped fresh mint
1 tsp wholegrain mustard
4 x 175g/6 oz lean leg of lamb steaks
1 rounded tsp cornflour
2 tbsp unsweetened orange juice
1 tbsp chopped fresh mint
Salt and pepper

Mix together the first four ingredients. Place lamb steaks in a non-metalic dish and cover with the orange juice mix. Leave to marinate 1 hour.

Pre-heat oven to 200°C/gas mark 6.

Remove lamb steaks from the marinade and transfer to a roasting tin. Reserve marinade. Bake steaks 15 minutes-20 minutes, or to your liking. Remove from oven and keep warm whilst making sauce.

Drain meat juices into a saucepan and add reserved marinade. Mix cornflour with 2 tbsp orange juice and stir into marinade. Bring to the boil and cook 3 minutes, stirring continuously, until sauce has reduced and thickened slightly. Add 1 tbsp chopped mint and season to taste.

Serve sauce with lamb steaks.

Serving suggestion

Serve each person with 1 lamb steak, quarter of the sauce, 150g/5 oz new potatoes, and "free" vegetables.

per serving : · · · · 380 ·

or 1 Main Meal

classic
Lower-fat Scotch Eggs

Makes 4 eggs

per Scotch egg   200   **8** 12

| 4 medium eggs, hard-boiled and cooled |
| 4 large low-fat sausages |
| 1 tsp mixed herbs |
| 1 medium slice wholemeal bread |
| A little skimmed milk |

Remove skins from sausages and mash in a bowl. Mix in the herbs.

Peel the hard-boiled eggs. Divide the sausage meat into 4 and wrap one portion around each egg.

Make the bread into crumbs. Dip each sausage-wrapped egg into a little skimmed milk and then into the breadcrumbs.

Bake on a rack over a baking tray approximately 30-40 minutes until the crumbs are crisp. Turn once or twice during cooking. Allow to cool and store in the fridge.

Serving suggestions

Serve 1 Scotch egg with "free" salad and 1 medium slice bread spread with low fat spread.

per serving :   300   **12** 12

or 1 Quick Meal

Serve 1 Scotch egg with "free" salad and 1 serving Posh Potato Salad (see "Lighter Bites" section).

per serving :   350   **14** 15

or 1 Main Meal

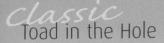
classic
Toad in the Hole

per serving   390   **16** (16)

or 1 Main Meal - see note below

8 large low-fat sausages
1 tsp oil
115g/4 oz plain flour
Pinch of salt
2 medium eggs, beaten
200ml/⅓ pint skimmed milk
"Free" vegetables to serve

Pre-heat oven to 220°C/gas mark 7.

Grill sausages well on one side and lightly on the other. Wipe on absorbent kitchen paper to remove any greasiness.

Rub oil around a roasting tin approximately 17cm x 27cm (7 inches x 11 inches) and put in the oven to get hot.

Sift flour and salt into a bowl. Make a well in the centre and gradually incorporate eggs and milk to make a smooth batter.

Remove tin from oven and immediately pour in batter. Arrange sausages in batter, well done side down. Bake 25-30 minutes until puffed and golden.

Serve one-quarter to each person, accompanied by "free" vegetables.

Note: *Many low-fat sausages contain around 100-110 calories/4 Checks and about 6g fat each. If you use very low fat sausages such as Wall's Lean Recipe or Marks & Spencer Count On Us, the count is reduced to*

per serving: 320   **13** (10)

or 1 Booster Main Meal

classic
Sausage & Tomato Pot

Serves 4

per serving   400 **16** (13)

or 1 Main Meal - see note below

225g/8 oz carrots
150g/5 oz onions
1 stick celery
2 x 400g cans tomatoes
1 beef or pork stock cube, e.g. Knorr
8 large low-fat sausages
900g/2 lb potatoes

Peel and slice carrots, onions and celery and put into a large saucepan together with the tomatoes and crumbled stock cube.

Bring to the boil, stirring now and again to dissolve stock cube fully. Reduce heat, cover and simmer until vegetables are tender.

Boil the potatoes and drain.

Meanwhile, grill the sausages then cut into chunks. Add sausages to the vegetables and tomatoes and simmer 10 minutes, adding a little water if necessary.

Serve each person with one-quarter of the boiled potatoes and one-quarter of the Sausage & Tomato Pot.

Note: *Many low-fat sausages contain around 100-110 calories/4 Checks and about 6g fat each. If you use very low fat sausages such as Wall's Lean Recipe or Marks & Spencer Count On Us (around 70 calories/3 Checks 3g fat or less, each) the count is reduced to*

per serving: 330 **13** (7)

or 1 Booster Main Meal

Classic
Corned Beef Crusty Top

Serves 1

per serving   320 **13** (10)

or 1 Booster Main Meal

1 small onion, chopped
85g/3 oz (quarter of 340g can) corned beef
200g canned tomatoes, chopped
Pinch of mixed herbs
50g/1¾ oz French bread
Spray oil
Pinch of garlic powder or 1 clove garlic
Pinch of mixed herbs
"Free" vegetables to serve

Pre-heat oven to 220°C/gas mark 7.

Cook onion in a small pan of water until soft, or microwave.

Cube the corned beef and place in an ovenproof dish together with the cooked onions, chopped tomatoes and pinch of mixed herbs.

Cut the bread into 3 or 4 slices to fit the dish. Spray lightly with oil and either sprinkle with garlic powder or cut the clove of garlic in half and rub the cut side over the bread. Sprinkle with mixed herbs and place on top of corned beef mixture.

Bake approximately 10-15 minutes, or until bread is crispy and golden. Serve with "free" vegetables.

classic
Savoury Pasties

per pasty   320 **13** (12)

or 1 Booster Main Meal

175g/6 oz self-raising flour
75g/2½ oz low-fat spread
2-3 tbsp cold water, as required
175g/6 oz lean minced beef
115g/4 oz peeled weight potato
115g/4 oz peeled weight swede/turnip
60g/2 oz peeled weight onion
Salt and pepper
Worcester sauce
Skimmed milk for brushing
"Free" vegetables to serve

Pre-heat oven to 200°C/gas mark 6.

Sift flour and salt together. Rub low-fat spread into flour until it resembles breadcrumbs. Add water, 1 tbsp at a time, and make into dough. Let pastry rest, covered, in the fridge ½ hour.

Cut potato and swede/turnip into small dice. Boil until tender and drain.

Chop onion finely and brown together with the mince. Cover and simmer 5-10 minutes until onion is soft. Stir potato and swede/turnip into mince. Remove from heat and season with salt, pepper and Worcester sauce to taste.

Roll out pastry into 4 circles, approximately 15cm/6 inches diameter, on a lightly floured board. Divide meat mixture between the 4 circles . Brush edges of circles with skimmed milk and crimp together to make pasty shapes. Prick with a fork, brush with a little skimmed milk and bake 25-30 minutes, or until crisp and golden.

Serve each person with 1 pasty accompanied by "free" vegetables. Alternatively, serve cold with "free" salad.

Classic
Liver & Pineapple Kebabs

Serves 1

per serving   150   **6**

75g/2½ oz lamb's liver
6 cubes pineapple canned in juice
2-3 tsp juice from canned pineapple
5-6 small button mushrooms
5-6 squares red or green pepper
5-6 thin wedges of onion
Spray oil

Cut liver into 6 squares. Thread onto skewers alternating with pineapple, mushroom, pepper and onion.

Sprinkle 2-3 tsp pineapple juice over ingredients to moisten. Spray lightly with oil and grill 5-8 minutes.

Serving suggestion

Serve kebabs with 60g/2 oz pitta bread and "free" salad.

per serving :   300   **12**

or 1 Quick Meal

Note: *Liver should not be eaten by anyone who is pregnant or likely to become pregnant.*

Meat-free Menu

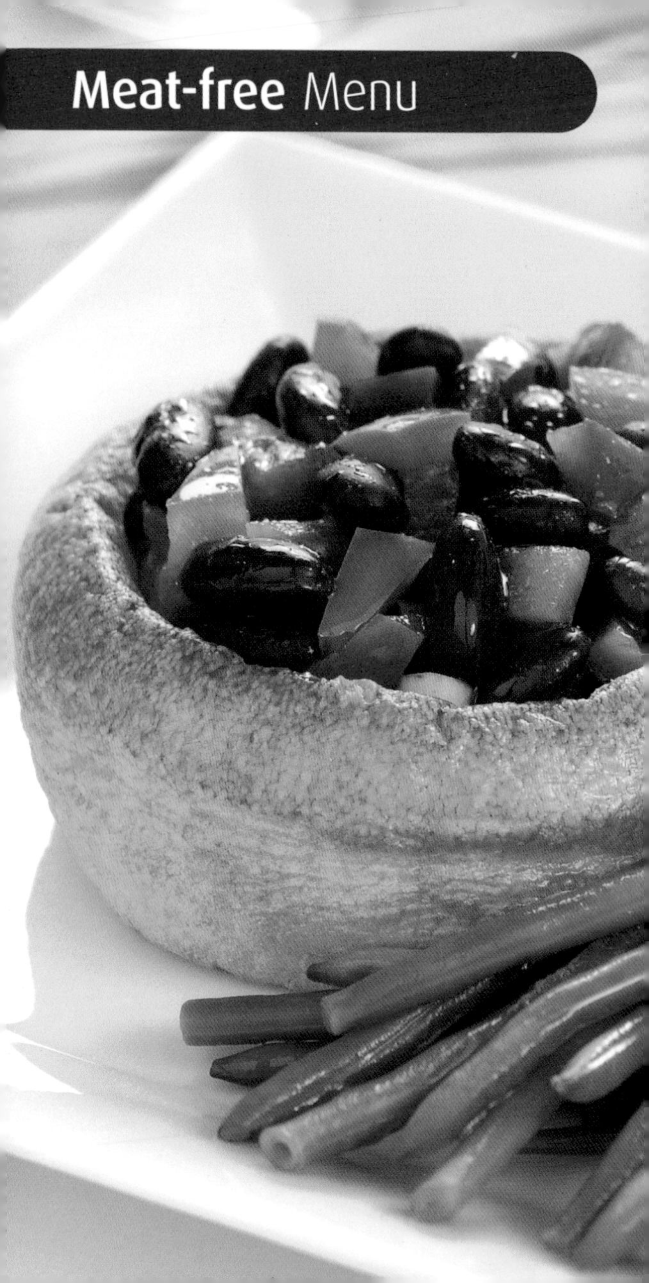

Vegetable Chilli Filled Yorkshires

Serves 2

per serving   350   **14** (11)

or 1 Booster Main Meal

---

1 medium onion, chopped
1 green pepper, chopped or a handful of frozen sliced mixed peppers
Spray oil
400-425g can kidney beans
400g can tomatoes
Pinch cumin
Pinch garlic powder
1 tsp chilli powder (or to taste)
1 Oxo vegetable cube
4 Aunt Bessie Large (not giant!) 4-minute Yorkshire Puddings*

Soften onion and peppers in a pan sprayed with oil, adding a little water now and again to prevent sticking.

Drain kidney beans and rinse. Add beans, tomatoes, cumin, garlic and chilli powder, and crumbled Oxo cube to the pan. Mix well and simmer gently 10-15 minutes to thicken sauce and allow flavours to develop.

Warm Yorkshire puddings 4 minutes according to pack instructions. Pour vegetable chilli into warmed Yorkshires and serve 2 to each person accompanied by green beans or other "free" vegetables.

* If using a different brand, each Yorkshire pudding should have around 100-110 calories or 4 Checks 4-5g fat.

Classic
Macaroni & Vegetable Cheese

Serves 1

per serving   300 **12** (5)

or 1 Quick Meal

45g/1½ oz short-cut macaroni
150g/5 oz prepared fresh or frozen "free" vegetables, e.g. broccoli or cauliflower or courgettes
1 rounded dspn cornflour
150ml/quarter-pint skimmed milk
30g/1 oz mature half-fat cheddar, grated
½ tsp mustard, or to taste
Salt and pepper
1 tomato, sliced

Cook the macaroni and vegetables together in lightly salted boiling water until tender. Drain and place in a heatproof dish.

Mix the cornflour with the milk in a small saucepan. Bring to the boil stirring continuously until sauce thickens. Stir in grated cheese, mustard and seasoning and cook 1 minute more.

Pour sauce over macaroni and vegetables and garnish with tomato slices. Brown under a hot grill.

Note: *For quickness, cheese sauce could be made by placing 3 heaped dessertspoons Bisto Cheese Sauce Granules into a measuring jug and stirring in boiling water up to the 175ml/6fl.oz mark. Calorie and Check values remain approximately the same, but fat grams go up to 10g.*

classic
Spicy Bean Burgers

per burger   75   **3** ❶

115g/4 oz carrots, coarsely grated
60g/2 oz onion, finely diced
1 stick celery, finely sliced
30g/1 oz red pepper, diced
425g can red kidney beans, drained and rinsed
1 tbsp tomato purée
¼ tsp chilli powder, or to taste
4 tsp fine oatmeal

Pre-heat oven to 200°C/gas mark 6.

Add carrots, onion, celery and pepper to some lightly salted boiling water and cook until onion and celery are softened. Drain.

Mash kidney beans. Stir in cooked vegetables, tomato purée and chilli powder. Mix well.

Shape mixture into 4 burgers and coat each with 1 tsp fine oatmeal. Use a fish slice to turn burgers over as mixture is quite soft. Place burgers onto a non-stick baking tray and bake 20-25 minutes, turning halfway through cooking.

Serving suggestion

Lightly toast a sesame seed topped burger bun. Place 1 burger on each half, topping each with 1 tsp burger relish. Serve with "free" salad.

per serving :   330   **13** ❹

or 1 Booster Main Meal
or 1 Quick Meal plus 1 Check

Jacket Potato
with Creamy Leeks

Serves 1

per serving   375 **15** **8**

or 1 Main Meal

275g/10 oz potato
2 rounded tbsp peas or petit pois
1 tsp low-fat spread
85g/3 oz trimmed weight leek, sliced
85g/3 oz extra light soft cheese
(e.g. Philadelphia Extra Light)
2-3 tbsp skimmed milk
Salt and pepper

Bake or microwave potato in it's jacket. Boil or microwave peas.

Melt low-fat spread in a saucepan and add leeks. Stir 1-2 minutes, cover and sweat gently a few minutes until soft. Stir in soft cheese, and skimmed milk to desired consistency. Stir and warm through. Season to taste.

Cut potato in half, pour over leek mixture and serve accompanied by peas.

classic

Savoury Cheese & Tomato Pudding

per serving   375 **15** (14)

or 1 Main Meal

2 medium slices wholemeal bread
2 tsp tomato purée
Spray oil
1 large tomato, sliced
Mixed herbs
30g/1 oz half-fat chedder, grated
2 tsp grated parmesan cheese
1 medium egg
Approx. 120ml/4 fl oz skimmed milk
½ tsp mild mustard
½ vegetable Oxo cube
"Free" vegetables or salad to serve

Pre-heat oven to 190°C/gas mark 5.

Spread bread with tomato purée and cut each slice into 4 triangles. Spray an ovenproof dish lightly with oil. Place 4 triangles in the base of the dish and top with half the tomato slices, a pinch of mixed herbs, about one-third of the grated cheddar and 1 tsp grated parmesan. Lay remaining bread, tomato slices and another pinch of herbs on top.

Lightly beat egg and make up to 150ml/¼ pint with skimmed milk. Stir in mustard and crumbled Oxo. Pour over bread and tomato layers and allow to stand 20 minutes. Sprinkle with remaining cheddar and parmesan.

Bake approximately 20 minutes, or until set and lightly browned. Serve either warm or cold with "free" vegetables or salad.

per serving   300 **13** 3

or 1 Quick Meal
or 1 Booster Main Meal

1 small onion, chopped
1 carrot, sliced
1 stick celery, sliced
60g/2 oz small cauliflower florets
175g/6 oz peeled and cubed potato
200g small can tomatoes
1 tsp yeast extract, e.g. Marmite
1 tsp mixed herbs
115g/4 oz cooked or canned butter beans, or other beans
1 medium slice wholemeal bread, made into crumbs

Pre-heat oven to 180°C/gas mark 4.

Cook onion, carrot, celery, cauliflower and potato in lightly salted boiling water until tender. Drain and transfer to an ovenproof casserole. Alternatively, cook covered in the microwave, with a little water, approximately 10 minutes.

Mix in tomatoes, yeast extract, and herbs. Stir in beans. Top with breadcrumbs and bake uncovered approximately 20-25 minutes.